D0579315

THOMAS *Edison*

Our People

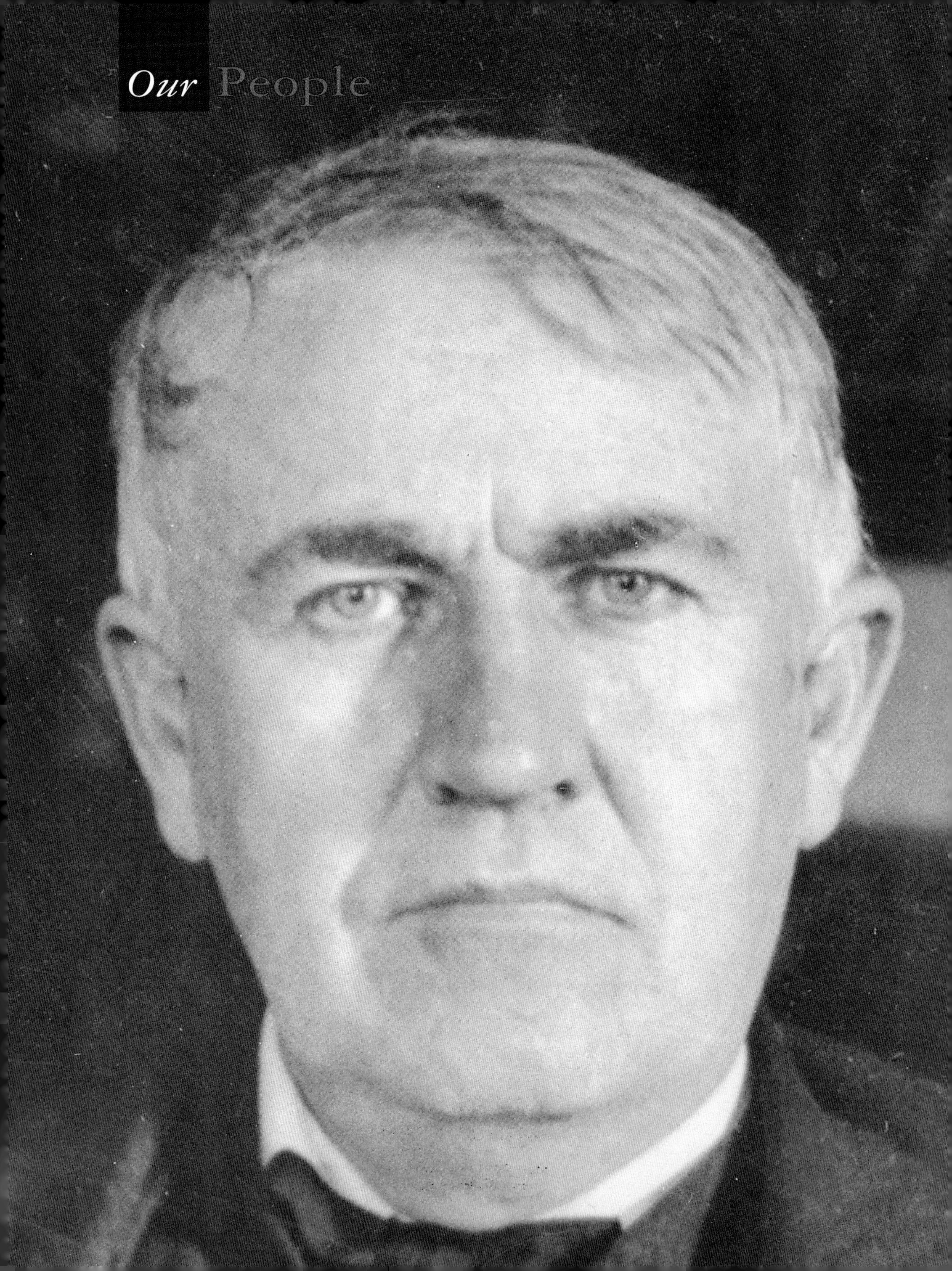

SPIRIT
of America®

THOMAS *Edison*

INVENTOR

By Cynthia Klingel and Robert B. Noyed

Content Adviser: Jack Stanley, Director, The Thomas Edison Memorial Tower and Menlo Park Museum, Edison, New Jersey

The
Child's
World

The Child's World®
Chanhassen, Minnesota

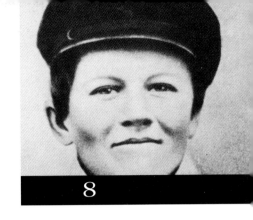

8

Thomas *Edison*

Published in the United States of America by *The Child's World*®
PO Box 326 • Chanhassen, MN 55317-0326 • 800-599-READ • www.childsworld.com

Acknowledgments
The Child's World®.: Mary Berendes, Publishing Director

Editorial Directions, Inc.: E. Russell Primm, Emily J. Dolbear, and Pam Rosenberg, Editors; Dawn Friedman, Photo Researcher; Linda S. Koutris, Photo Selector; Sarah E. De Capua, Copy Editor; Susan Ashley, Proofreader; Tim Griffin, Indexer

Photo
Cover: U.S. Department of the Interior, National Park Service, Edison National Historic Site; Bettmann/Corbis: 6, 22; Hulton-Deutsch Collection/Corbis: 12; Corbis: 20, 23, 24, 27; Hulton Archive/Getty Images: 18; North Wind Picture Archives: 10, 11; U.S. Department of the Interior, National Park Service, Edison National Historic Site: 2, 7, 8, 9, 13, 14, 15, 16, 17, 19 top and bottom, 21, 25, 28.

Library of Congress Cataloging-in-Publication Data
Klingel, Cynthia Fitterer.
  Thomas Edison : inventor / by Cynthia Klingel and Robert B. Noyed.
    p. cm.
"Spirit of America."
Summary: A biography of the inventor who changed the world in which he lived with such revolutionary inventions as the phonograph, electric lighting, and motion pictures.
Includes bibliographical references and index.
  ISBN 1-56766-449-0 (Library Bound : alk. paper) *33628032 11/05*
1. Edison, Thomas A. (Thomas Alva), 1847–1931—Juvenile literature.
2. Inventors—United States—Biography—Juvenile literature. [1.
Edison, Thomas A. (Thomas Alva), 1847–1931. 2. Inventors.] I. Noyed,
Robert B. II. Title.
  TK140.E3 K55 2003
  621.3'092—dc21

                    2002151723

Contents

Chapter ONE	*The Young Scientist*	6
Chapter TWO	*Journey to Menlo Park*	12
Chapter THREE	*Phonographs and Lightbulbs*	18
Chapter FOUR	*Lighting Up the Country*	22
	Time Line	29
	Glossary Terms	30
	For Further Information	31
	Index	32

The Young Scientist

THOMAS EDISON ONCE SAID, "GENIUS IS ONE percent **inspiration** and 99 percent **perspiration**." His ideas for inventions were important, but his hard work was what made them. Throughout Edison's life, he received more than 1,000 **patents**. Many of his inventions changed people's lives.

Thomas Edison in his lab in 1901

Thomas Alva Edison was born on February 11, 1847, in Milan, Ohio. Edison's parents called him Al. Samuel and Nancy Edison had six children before Thomas was born.

Three of the Edison children died when they were young. When Thomas was born, his brother and two sisters were teenagers. He played by himself much of the time.

When Thomas was about seven years old, he became sick with scarlet fever. As a result, he lost some of his hearing. He also suffered from inflammation of the bones inside his ears. This, too, made him lose some of his hearing. Thomas lived for the rest of his life with some hearing loss.

In 1854, the Edison family moved to Port Huron, Michigan. Thomas began attending school there. Because he could not hear well, he had to ask many questions. His teacher did not think Thomas was smart. Thomas was frustrated at school. He stayed for only a few months. His

Samuel Edison (top, left) was Thomas Edison's father. Nancy Edison (below) was Thomas Edison's mother.

mother was trained as a teacher. She decided to teach her son at home.

Thomas loved to read about science **experiments**. He enjoyed creating things. His mother let him set up a **laboratory** in their basement. Thomas Edison spent many hours in his lab.

Edison as a young boy

The Edisons did not have a lot of money. Thomas got a job to help earn money. When he was 12 years old, he began working on the railroad line between Port Huron and Detroit. Instead of staying home to do his schoolwork, Thomas took a job as a candy butcher. Candy butchers were people who sold newspapers and snacks to people on the trains.

Early in the morning, he got on the train for the three-hour trip to Detroit. After spending all day in Detroit, he returned home on the

Edison sold candy and newspapers on the train that was pulled by this locomotive.

train at night. During the day, he spent his time reading books at the library. He also went to the **telegraph** office. The telegraph operators **fascinated** him.

Thomas Edison spent some of the money he earned to buy science books. The train conductor also let him set up another laboratory in an empty railroad car. He worked on his experiments while he waited for the train to return at the end of each day.

One day in 1862, Thomas performed a heroic deed. The stationmaster's son was playing on the railroad tracks. A boxcar was rolling toward the boy. Thomas ran and

Interesting Fact

▶ While selling papers from the train, young Edison decided to print his own newspaper while riding the train from town to town. It was called the *Weekly Herald*. It was the first newspaper ever written for train travel.

Telegraph operators work in a Western Union telegraph office.

pulled the boy off the tracks. He saved the boy's life. James MacKenzie, the stationmaster, knew of Thomas's interest in telegraphy. To thank Thomas for saving his son's life, MacKenzie taught Thomas how to become a telegraph operator.

Thomas became very good at operating the telegraph. When he was 16 years old, he took a job at a telegraph office in Port Huron. He worked as a telegraph operator for more than six years. Thomas liked working at night so he could do his science experiments during the day.

10

TELEGRAPHY IS THE PROCESS OF USING A TELEGRAPH TO SEND AND RECEIVE messages. A telegraph is a machine that people use to tap out a message. The message is sent through wires over short or long distances. The telegraph was first used on May 24, 1844. It was invented by Samuel F. B. Morse. Morse made up a code of dots and dashes that stand for different letters of the alphabet. For example, the letter A is • – (dot/dash).

When Thomas Edison was a boy, there were no telephones or televisions. Telegraphs were the usual way to send messages quickly over long distances. The telegraph changed the way people shared information. People did not have to wait for letters to arrive. Newspapers could get information right away.

The telegraph was important until the 1940s. Then, telephones and televisions replaced the telegraph as ways to send and receive information.

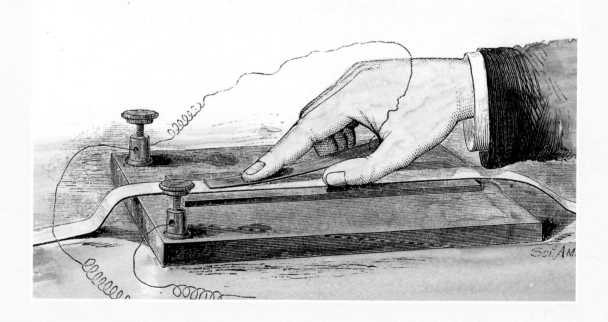

Chapter TWO

Journey to Menlo Park

Thomas Edison moved
to Boston when he was
21 years old.

IN 1868, WHEN THOMAS EDISON WAS 21 YEARS old, he moved to Boston, Massachusetts. He started working at Western Union, the largest telegraph company in the United States. Edison liked Boston because many of the best inventors and scientists lived there.

Edison spent much of his time studying electricity. Electricity is a form of energy. He used the money he earned as a telegraph operator to buy the book *Experimental Researches in Electricity*. It was written by Michael Faraday, an English scientist. Edison was very interested in the experiments described in the book. The book inspired Edison to become an inventor.

Edison spent his free time performing experiments. He had many ideas for new inventions. In 1869, Edison received his first patent. It was for an electrical vote counter. The invention allowed **politicians** to push buttons for a "yes" or "no" vote. The invention worked well, but no one was interested in buying it. Edison later said that the experience taught him not to invent things that people did not want!

In 1869, Thomas Edison got a job with Samuel Law's Gold and Stock Reporting Company in New York City. He arrived in the city with no money. With no place to stay, Edison slept in the basement of the office building where he worked. One day, while Edison was in the office, the stock ticker stopped working and no one knew how to fix it. Businesses used stock tickers to send prices from the stock market. Everyone was upset because they could not work without the ticker. Edison had a natural talent for fixing machines. He noticed that a spring had come loose in the stock ticker. He

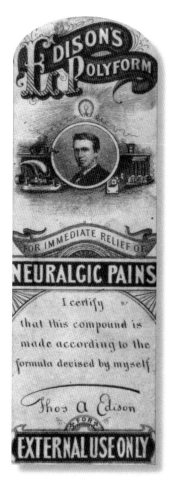

The company that made this medicine for pain paid Thomas Edison for the use of his name on its product.

Interesting Fact

▶ The motion picture camera was invented by Edison and his staff in 1891.

Stock tickers were used by businesses to keep track of prices on the stock market.

said he could fix it. He put the spring back in place and the stock ticker began working again. The vice president of the company saw this. Edison was made manager of the New York branch of the company that same day!

Thomas Edison's next invention was a better stock ticker machine. Edison sold his ideas for the better stock ticker for $40,000. This was a huge amount of money at that time. He quit his job and used the money to set up a workshop in Newark, New Jersey. He hired more than 300 people to work there. It was in the Newark workshop that Edison worked to create better telegraph machines.

One of the people who worked in Edison's workshop was Mary Stillwell. She was a 16-year-old assistant. She helped others with their work. Edison was always busy in the workshop, but he wanted to get to know Mary. However, he was very shy. He did not know how to start talking with her, so he would just walk up to her and stare.

Mary told him that he made her nervous when he did that. Edison replied by asking, "Do you like me, girlie?" They became friends. Within a few weeks Edison asked, "Will you marry me, girlie?" Mary said yes, and they were married on December 25, 1871. Thomas and Mary Edison had three children—Marion, Thomas Alva Junior, and William.

Edison's work continued to be one of the most important things in his life. In 1876, Western Union hired him to improve the telephone invented by Alexander Graham Bell. At about the same time, Edison moved his workshop to Menlo Park, New Jersey. He built a large laboratory, which he called the Invention Factory. Edison told everyone, "We will come up with a small thing every ten days and a big thing about every six months."

Mary Stillwell married Thomas Edison in 1871.

Edison spent much of his time in the workshop. Often he would work for three days straight and then take three days off. He expected those who worked with him to work long hours as well. However, Edison knew that he and his team could not continue to work and be creative without having some fun. The workers in Menlo Park had their own band. Sometimes Edison would lead parades around the workshop. Other times, Edison would rent a boat and they would go fishing.

Edison (seated next to the window on the right) and his team in their lab

16

WOULD YOU LIKE TO BE AN inventor? Inventions can happen in many different ways. Sometimes they come from making mistakes in the laboratory. Sometimes inventions come out of careful, hard work to solve a problem. Some inventions make a lot of money and help many people.

Inventing something can be exciting. It is also important that the inventor get a patent for the invention. The United States government gives patents through the U.S. Patent and Trademark Office in Washington, D.C.

An inventor must give a lot of information about the invention. First, the U.S. Patent and Trademark Office makes sure that no one else already has a patent for the invention or any part of the invention. Then the inventor is given a patent. This means that the inventor is the only person who can make, use, or sell that invention in the United States for a set period of time.

Chapter THREE

Phonographs and Lightbulbs

OVER TIME, THOMAS EDISON BECAME A WELL-known inventor. Newspaper reporters visited his workshop to see his inventions. By 1877, he was finding great success.

Edison used his experience with the telegraph to improve the telephone. He invented the carbon button **transmitter**. This made a voice on Edison's telephone easier to hear than on Bell's telephone. Jay Gould, who later gained control of the Western Union Telegraph Company, bought Edison's telephone for over $100,000.

In July 1877, Edison discovered a way to record sounds. While experimenting with a telephone mouthpiece, he put a needle in the center of it and cut a slot on either side. He folded waxed paper into a V shape. He placed it against the needle, and pulled it through

Edison's Motograph telephone

the slots on either side of the mouthpiece while saying "Mary had a little lamb." When he pulled the waxed paper through the mouthpiece again, he heard sound played back. The words were not clear, but Edison was excited. This was the first time ever that sound was recorded!

Edison's experiments with recording sound led to the development of this early phonograph.

Over the next few months, Edison and his team worked on ways to improve this discovery. On December 6, 1877, they were ready to officially test the "sound writer," which was the first **phonograph**. Edison read the poem "Mary Had a Little Lamb" into the machine. He turned the **cylinder** on the phonograph. He heard his voice played back. Their design was a success! He was ready to share this amazing invention with the world.

Thomas Edison with his cylinder phonograph

The next day, Edison brought his phonograph to the offices of *Scientific American* magazine. He placed the phonograph on the editor's desk and pressed a button. The phonograph introduced itself to the editor. The editor could not believe what he heard! This was truly the greatest invention of

President Rutherford B. Hayes invited Edison to the White House to demonstrate the phonograph.

Edison's life. He received a patent for his phonograph and for his ideas for ways to record sound.

News of Edison's phonograph was in every newspaper in the country. Edison was asked by Congress to show them how his invention worked. President Rutherford B. Hayes invited Edison to the White House so he could see the invention for himself. Thomas Edison stayed at the White House until 3 A.M. because he, the president, and the president's wife and children were having so much fun playing with the phonograph.

After the phonograph, Thomas Edison began working on another project. This time, he wanted to improve the **incandescent** light-bulb. He had been working with electricity for many years. He began thinking about how to create light using electricity. At the time, candles and gas lamps lit most homes. Gas lit the street lamps in many cities, too. These lamps were dangerous because the gas often leaked and had a strong odor. Some streets were lit by an early kind of electric lamp called an arc lamp. These were dangerous and noisy.

Many other inventors were also trying to

create a lightbulb. None of them had been successful at making a lightbulb that could be used every day. Edison read books about their experiments. He learned as much as he could about the problems they had. Edison was sure that his lightbulb would work.

Edison wanted to finish this project as soon as he could. Many people worked on the lightbulb in his laboratory. They tried many different ways to make it work. Edison experimented with different filaments in the lightbulb. The filament is the material inside a lightbulb that glows and gives off light. After many tries, Edison and his team found an idea that worked. On October 21, 1879, they connected the lightbulb to the electric current. The bulb lit up! The bulb burned for about 14 hours. They kept working to make the lightbulb burn longer.

This Edison effect bulb was one of the first steps toward modern electronics.

On New Year's Eve, Edison invited people to come to Menlo Park. Thousands of people were there when he hit a switch and lit up the night. Newspapers carried the news of Edison's success with the lightbulb. The electric lightbulb would soon change the lives of people throughout the United States.

Chapter FOUR

Lighting Up the Country

Edison moved to New York to begin working on America's first power plant.

PEOPLE FOUND EDISON'S IMPROVED LIGHTBULB amazing. However, his team kept working on the lightbulb to make it even better. The next step for Edison was to create a way to bring electricity to many people at one time.

Edison moved to New York to begin work on creating America's first electric power plant. His goal was to provide light for the entire city. At that time, no city in the United States had an electrical supply system. Edison and his team had to create all the parts of the system. They designed the generators that

A power plant on the East River in New York City

made the electricity. They created the underground wiring system that carried the electricity to homes and businesses. They also created the meters to measure how much electricity each customer used.

Other companies also wanted to make electricity for the city of New York. Edison convinced city officials to use his system, though. On September 4, 1882, Edison's power plant on Pearl Street began generating electricity. It was a huge success. Edison opened a second power plant a short time later in Wisconsin. This plant used water from the Fox River to electricity. It was America's first hydroelectric power plant.

Interesting Fact

The Pearl Street power plant once experienced a power leak. Electricity traveled to the manhole covers throughout New York City. When the horses that were pulling carriages stepped on the manhole covers with their metal horseshoes they received electric shocks. The shocked, fearful horses created quite a spectacle that day.

Edison's kinetoscope led to the development of the motion picture projector.

Edison set up his own electric companies in the United States and in Europe. His success with electric lights made him rich.

In 1884, Edison's wife Mary became ill. She died on August 9. Edison was left to raise their three young children on his own. Two years later, Edison met and married Mina Miller. She was about 20 years old when they met. Together, they had three children.

After the perfection of the electric light-bulb, Edison kept working hard. Much of his work in later years was used to create motion pictures and improve the phonograph.

In 1929, Edison's health began to fail. He died on October 18, 1931, at the age of 84. During his life, Thomas Edison and his companies were granted 1,093 patents—more than any other inventor. Edison used a team of scientists instead of working by himself. This made him one of the most successful inventors of all time. His inventions changed forever the way people live and work. Our lives are easier today because of Edison's hard work and creativity.

*Thomas Edison in his lab
on his 74th birthday*

EDISON'S FIRST WIFE WAS MARY STILLWELL EDISON. MARY WAS BORN on September 6, 1855, in Newark, New Jersey. After marrying on December 25, 1871, they had three children—Marion, Thomas Jr., and William—over the next 13 years. During that time, Mary was liked and respected by the men who worked with Edison. She often brought lunch and dinner to Edison and "the boys" when they were busy in the lab. In 1884, Mary died. She was only 28 years old. Edison was deeply saddened by her death. His long hours in the lab had kept him from spending as much time with her as he would have liked.

On February 24, 1886, Edison remarried. His second wife was Mina Miller. Mina was born on July 6, 1865. Her father was also a famous inventor named Lewis Miller. When he first heard of

Edison's phonograph, he believed that it was a fake. He and a minister, John Heyl Vincent, traveled to Menlo Park to prove that Edison's phonograph did not work. When they arrived, Edison invited Vincent to record his voice. Vincent recited Bible verses very quickly so that no one hiding nearby could repeat what he was saying. When Edison played back Vincent's voice, Miller knew the phonograph was real. Lewis Miller and Thomas Edison became good friends.

Mina and Edison had three children of their own. Their names were Madeleine, Charles, and Theodore.

1847 Thomas Edison is born on February 11 in Milan, Ohio.

1863 Edison begins working as a telegraph operator.

1869 Edison receives his first patent for the electrical vote recorder.

1870 Edison starts a company that makes stock tickers.

1871 Edison marries Mary Stillwell on December 25.

1874 Edison's design for an improved telegraph is completed.

1876 The Menlo Park laboratory is built.

1877 Edison designs a better telephone and invents the phonograph.

1879 Edison and his team produce the first practical electric lightbulb.

1882 The first electric power plant, built by Edison, opens in New York City.

1884 Mary Stillwell Edison dies.

1886 Edison marries Mina Miller and builds a lab in West Orange, New Jersey.

1891 The motion picture camera is invented by Edison and his team.

1894 Thomas Edison makes the world's first motion picture.

1912 Edison introduces the disc phonograph.

1928 Edison receives the Medal of Honor from the U.S. Congress.

1929 Edison is honored on the 50th anniversary of the incandescent light on October 21.

1931 Edison dies on October 18.

Glossary Terms

engineers (en-je-NEERZ)
Engineers specialize in the science of making nature and energy useful to people. Thomas Edison worked with many engineers in his laboratory.

generators (JEN-a-rate-ers)
Generators are machines that change mechanical energy to electrical energy. Edison and his team of scientists invented generators to create electricity.

hydroelectric (hy-dro-i-LEK-trik)
Harnessing the power of moving water creates hydroelectric energy. Edison used the moving water of the Fox River to generate electricity in Wisconsin.

incandescent (in-kan-DES-ent)
Something that is incandescent gives off light produced by intense heat. Edison worked to create a better incandescent light bulb.

inspiration (in-spe-RAY-shun)
An inspiration is something that influences the mind or emotions.

laboratory (LAB-ra-tor-ee)
A laboratory is a place where experiments are done. Thomas Edison had a laboratory at Menlo Park.

patent (PAT-nt)
A patent is document that says a certain person or company is the only one with the right to make or sell an invention for a certain number of years. Edison earned many patents over his lifetime.

perspiration (pur-spuh-RAY-shun)
Perspiration is another word for sweating. When people do hard work they often perspire or sweat.

phonograph (FOH-na-graf)
A phonograph is a machine that reproduces the sounds recorded on a grooved disk. Phonographs are also called record players.

politicians (pol-uh-TISH-unz)
People who are active in political parties and conduct the business of government are called politicians.

telegraph (TEL-uh-graf)
The telegraph is a device that uses electricity to send coded messages over wires. Edison worked as a telegraph operator when he was a young man.

transmitter (trans-MIT-ter)
The part of the telephone that picks up sound waves and sends the sounds over the wires is called the transmitter. Thomas Edison worked to improve the transmitter on Alexander Graham Bell's telephone.

For Further INFORMATION

Web Sites

Visit our homepage for lots of links about Thomas Edison and his inventions:
http://www.childsworld.com/links.html

Note to Parents, Teachers, and Librarians:
We routinely verify our Web links to make sure they're safe,
active sites—so encourage your readers to check them out!

Books

Adler, David A. *A Picture Book of Thomas Alva Edison.* New York: Holiday House, 1999.

Ford, Carin T. *Thomas Edison: Inventor.* Berkeley Heights, N.J.: Enslow Publishers, 2002.

Williams, Brian. *Thomas Alva Edison.* Chicago: Heinemann Library, 2002.

Places to Visit or Contact

Edison National Historic Site
To tour Edison's West Orange laboratory and Glenmont, Edison's home
Edison National Historic Site
Main Street and Lakeside Avenue
West Orange, NJ 07052
973/736-0550

Thomas Alva Edison Memorial Tower and Menlo Park Museum
To see some of Edison's inventions and products sold by the Thomas A. Edison Company
37 Christie Street
Edison, NJ 08820
732/248-7298

Index

Bell, Alexander Graham, 15
Boston, Massachusetts, 12

candy butchers, 8
carbon button transmitter, 18

Edison, Charles (son), 28
Edison, Madeleine (daughter), 28
Edison, Marion (daughter), 15, 28
Edison, Mary Stillwell (wife), 14–15, 23, 26, 28
Edison, Mina (wife), 23, 26, 28
Edison, Nancy (mother), 6–7, 8
Edison, Samuel (father), 6–7
Edison, Theodore (son), 23, 28
Edison, Thomas Alva
  birth of, 6
  as candy butcher, 8–9
  childhood of, 7
  death of, 27
  education of, 7–8
  patents of, 6, 13, 20, 23, 26
  as telegraph operator, 10, 12
  threats against, 27
  work habits of, 15–16
Edison, Thomas Alva, Jr. (son), 15, 28
Edison, William (son), 15, 28
electric power plants, 23–25
electrical wiring, 24
electricity, 12, 20, 22, 24, 25
electricity usage meters, 24
Experimental Researches in Electricity
  (Michael Faraday), 12–13

Faraday, Michael, 12
filaments, 21

generators, 23
Gold and Stock Reporting Company, 13–14
Gould, Jay, 18

Hayes, Rutherford B., 20
hydroelectric power plants, 25

incandescent lightbulb, 20–21, 22, 26
Invention Factory, 15

Law, Samuel, 13
lightbulb, 20–21, 22, 26

MacKenzie, James, 10, 16
Menlo Park, New Jersey, 15, 16, 21, 28
Milan, Ohio, 6
Miller, Lewis, 28
Miller, Mina. See Edison, Mina.
Morse, Samuel F. B., 11
motion picture cameras, 13, 26

New York, New York, 13, 14, 23, 24
Newark, New Jersey, 14

patents, 6, 13, 17, 20, 23, 26
Pearl Street power plant, 25
phonograph, 18–20
Port Huron, Michigan, 7
power plants, 23–25

Scientific American magazine, 19
sound recordings, 18–20
Stillwell, Mary. See Edison, Mary Stillwell.
stock ticker machines, 14

telegraph machines, 9, 11, 14
telephone, 15, 18

U.S. Patent and Trademark Office, 17

Vincent, John Heyl, 23
voting machines, 13

Weekly Herald newspaper, 9
Western Union Telegraph Company, 12, 15, 18